THE STRINGS ARE LIGHTNING AND HOLD YOU IN

THE STRINGS
ARE LIGHTNING
AND HOLD YOU IN

POEMS

CHEE BROSSY

TUPELO PRESS
North Adams, Massachusetts

Library of Congress Cataloging-in-Publication Data
Identifiers: LCCN 2022030930 | ISBN 9781946482761 (paperback)
Subjects: LCGFT: Poetry.
Classification: LCC PS3602.R6474 S77 2022 | DDC 811/.6--dc23/eng/20220722
LC record available at https://lccn.loc.gov/2022030930
ISBN-13: 978-1-946482-76-1

Cover and text design by Howard Klein.
Cover art: "Designs of Creation" by Tso Yazzy / Chester Kahn (1936-2019).
Used by permission.

First paperback edition November 2022

Tupelo Press
P.O. Box 1767
North Adams, Massachusetts 01247
(413) 664-9611 / Fax: (413) 664-9711
editor@tupelopress.org / www.tupelopress.org

Tupelo Press is an award-winning independent literary press that publishes fine fiction,
non-fiction, and poetry in books that are a joy to hold as well as read. Tupelo Press is a
registered 501(c)(3) nonprofit organization, and we rely on public support to carry out
our mission of publishing extraordinary work that may be outside the realm of the large
commercial publishers. Financial donations are welcome and are tax deductible.

NATIONAL
ENDOWMENT
FOR THE ARTS

This project is supported in part by an award from the National Endowment for the Arts.

ACKNOWLEDGMENTS

I thank the editors of the following publications in which some of these poems have appeared, sometimes in earlier forms and under different titles:

Denver Quarterly, Narrative Magazine, Taos Journal of Poetry and Art, AGNI, Colorado Review, Copper Nickel, American Indian Culture and Research Journal, Prairie Schooner, Sentence Magazine, Toe Good Poetry and *Red Ink Magazine.*

Thank you to all the authors of *Navajo Stories of the Long Walk Period* for sharing your accounts so that we honor and remember. That book, like the stories from my own family, brought to life that troubled past and made it real. Some of those stories inspired poems in this book.

CONTENTS

INTRODUCTION

Diné poet Chee Brossy's brilliant debut poetry collection begins with "The Thawing of the World," a story of emergence in which "we climb out, / starlight vapor in our lungs, straining to breathe / after our long climb through the reeds." These starlight-touched creatures, the Diné, are the subjects of *The Strings Are Lightning and Hold Us In.*

Brossy brings to the poetry time spent as a journalist, a writer of short fiction, and an athlete, a young man raised on the Navajo Nation, rooted in Diné values and language, but one who has also traveled and studied and lived off the rez. These are poems from a man speaking among friends and relations. It is also a book about community and forgiveness and welcome: 'the boy has returned from a long journey,/ summer sheep-herd, from college, from an unhappy marriage. / We say, Boy, you've come back." History and tribal knowledge appear naturally in these poems, as do the pleasures of life on the reservation—the food, the light, the air, the sights and sounds and smells.

Poems are made, first of all, of language, and Brossy's care with language— actually several languages, including Diné Bizaad, English, and Spanish—is evident throughout. Formally diverse, the book includes prose poems in blocks and in paragraphic stanzas, long line and short line poems, poems that tell stories and poems that resist the notion that we can know what led to what and why. A common procedure is to let events and images rub against each other to see what might be revealed. One might call this process *quilting*, as in the poem of that title, which begins "Four children play WWE in a patch of dirt," then connects a child's fort, family gardening, a bomber flying over a reservation school, the brutality of the Navajo Long Walk as commemorated in a quilt, a comic book artist whose superheroes look white, and a father chopping wood.

And there are many such quilts in the book: The quilt of history—the Long Walk, boarding schools, border town violence, relocation—and the quilts made of family relationships, intertribal relationships, urban Diné and reservation Diné, younger Diné drifting from tribal ways while others participate in community life and learn the language even as they live lives off the reservation. Brossy's approach throughout is largely non-judgmental. Maybe it's his journalism training, but he seems most interested in *seeing* the world in all its quilted complexity: "The new punk rockers wail in Gorman Hall while the C-W dance thumps along next door in Nakai."

Cultural knowledge is woven organically into the poems—a man pulls his hair out, a process that will "trigger other ills," another man files a chainsaw chain seeking a particular angle, "an angle that would be named in the language, the lean of a horse's shadow at sunset would be the name." But the transmission of cultural knowledge is imperfect, endangered (sometimes comically so): "At the rodeo grounds the queen gives her acceptance speech / in Navajo. Was that a story about her grandparents? Her dog?"

The magnificent prose poem sequence "Burntwater," which ends the book, has as its source material a recorded conversation with Brossy's grandfather. In this prose poem, Brossy employs all the strategies he has developed—disjunction, association, modified syntax—to translate a world that cannot quite be translated. After a series of wrenching stories, the poem and the book end, appropriately, with a young Diné man and his grandfather in a hogan, but a hogan embedded in the modern world: "We'll stop here today. To the south the freeway rumbles trucks haul refrigerators and pipes. On the windowsill the metal stamps and thin brushes sprout from rusted cans. It's cold. Even with the sun shining through the skylight I'll have to build a fire." I can't help thinking that there's a metaphorical connection between that fire and this book.

—Jon Davis, author of *Above the Bejeweled City*

THE THAWING OF THE WORLD

At the thawing of the world, moss comes first,
then reeds, then grasshoppers, then glistening cicadas
chewing through a long hibernation.
          Then we climb out,

starlight vapor in our lungs, straining to breathe
after our long climb through the reeds.
Red spiders crawl from tin cans
          and weave the story's tapestries.

In Vietnam, the youths have returned, set up shop
as DJs, street artists, bakers
paving poems into novels.

In our fortress canyon we harvest apricots,
find it difficult to give them to our neighbors.
Crows light on cottonwoods and caw,
          admonishing.

Ten years pass and still you wake
from nightmares, having succeeded only
in scraping the frosty layer of frozen meat
          with a fingernail.

Leave counting to those who watch the stars.
We are visited when the clouds dip low
around cliffs, and sound deadens,
          shouts swallowed

into throats. Fog: protection breathed in for sudden storms.
The turtle tries, is always trying, lifetimes trying,
and then emerges, the world on his back.
When we have spent what is allotted,
      combed smoke

through our hair, twisted and tied the tassels—black, red,
black-red—copper pipes soldered against leaking,
the gifts will come, mailed years in advance,
      and falling tone—

that is the best time for it. As in Vietnam,
the boy has returned from a long journey,
summer sheep-herd, from college, from an unhappy marriage.
      We say, Boy, you've come back.

OWL AND THE SABER

Bíhoosh'aah: learning, to learn, I am learning something—(*ł'aah): to push a solid, round object (SrO) and thereby make space within yourself for a language, system, skill.

In Mexico, husband and wife are *love* around a dinner table. Pass the soup of shrimp, my love, administer mango yogurt, my love, plait my hair, mi amor, give me your scalp-scent, for tonight I desire to walk the festival's streets, to roam the Zócalo, to traffic, my hands full when a salesman strums his classical guitar—Handmade, he will say, just for you.

They tell me Indians will be out tonight. I will have their corn stew with chile and lime. Let's forget others we have called *love*, forget we ever knew them—conocer: to know, to have known, to be saturated with.

South of Socorro, in the Fearing Time, a woman escaped her Spanish-Mexican enslavers—tú la conoces. Travelling only at night, she encountered wolves and fought them with a cavalry saber. Se escapó. On the third night of running, of praying—sodilzin—an owl hooted and she stopped. Her next step would have been over the precipice. Who knows how far she would have fallen, how deep the canyon goes, if into trees, rocks, or water? She felt gravity looming. But for the owl and saber she would have fallen into wolves that night—to know, to have known, to be familiar with.

THE BOW IS RAINBOW

At the powwow we wait, wind blurring
the swinging lights, fighting our appetites,
for the Midnight Special.

Water: yarn-speckle caught in a weaving,
black triangles arrayed row upon row,
an oxidized swirl recessed into silver,

the blue corners of an ocher rug. When
did you begin? I want to know the *instant*
you began loving her.

But nodding boughs of spruce,
creaking stands of oak,
juniper berries sweet yet
and bursting in my mouth.

Whalebone settling, mastodon ivory
in the gift shop, your whole being in play.
Last time we talked you were headstrong.

Remember: Discipline! Respect!
Chile seeds cough in the frying pan,
smoke the house. We calcify in our shells,

critiquing our rival's address—
Does it *look* like a poem? Winding your way
into the canyon most things you can eat.

When my friend says *separation*,
we carry on about building houses,
me, sadly, trying to hide it.

Her last presence, the leafy houseplant
yellowing without water,
has been emptied from its hanging pot,

dumped in the yard. A shame not to know its name.
The brown grasshopper tastes of roasted piñon,
but I'm afraid of its spiky legs.

This is a windup bird, brass wings and ivory beak.
The mechanism wood and sinew,
wax and copper wire, wrapped and unwrapping.
Like the coast, we are prone to disaster,

to losing eyelashes, to thinning eyebrows,
to a soft, kind belly.
So we cling to an exact number of planets,
to the Earth Our Mother.

Little boy, when I held you
before the swaddling, your eyes came loose.
I wanted somehow to ease your red-stained eyes.

Cradleboard: the bow is rainbow,
the blanket, clouds.
The strings are lightning and hold you in.

HOMEMADE ICE CREAM

What I didn't say:
The escaping woman was pregnant.

Sitting on a bench at the Railyard,
my expectant friend listens to live music.
Someone sells homemade ice cream
out of a deep, frosty bin.
Look at it move, she says.
When the music gets too loud it moves.
She leans back so sun shines
on her rounded T-shirt.
But I'm too scared to touch it.
It's crazy, she says. Did you see?
I don't know what I saw.

If we sacrifice our children
for the good of the People what then?
Are we selfish or caring?

Because the woman with the saber
had no milk, she couldn't care for her baby.
No milk, no food to make it.
If they don't live to smile
with unrepeatable joy, at mother
behind the camera, sitting
on auntie and uncle's lap.
It's easy to be afraid.

When are the dances?
Already! she says. Where were you?
I'd like some ice cream, but it will take

too long. Already we shout
over the screaming electric guitar.
I've got to go, I say, even though I don't.
She looks disappointed, Already?
Waiting through this act for the next.

We wrap our children in our arms,
squeeze them as they squirm from us,
dress them in winter coats,
button their little Hawaiian shirts.
They jump into pools awaiting our catch,
smiling big until the splash makes them
blink because they had our milk.

Looking back, my friend has turned
to her sister, arranging who will wait
for homemade ice cream.

KUH

Shoulder pads swallow necks, make it difficult

to genuflect in a muddy, grassless field.
A girlfriend screams I hate you,

crying in your arms, smearing eye shadow on your
white tuxedo shirt. Is isit? A man stutters

through a prayer, his eyes bulge to get the kay out

kuh cancer kuh colostomy bag kuh Kalispell
kuh condom kuh cake cream cheese frosting

kuh késhjéé' kuh come you're like that,
running away from your country, your language

to Phoenix, to Tulsa, to San Bernardino.

Romance language: love, death, ache,
as when the Mexican lady calls her husband

of thirty years mi amor, or simply amor,
around the plastic-covered cena table.

We waited for késhjéé' shoegame to begin
díidigíí ours, the cowboy boots buried in dirt,

just the side-pulls showing, yucca counters
laid beside them in a bundle. But no one

took charge. Some advice: quit waiting for singers.
Sometimes they're at the casino, or lured

to Tent Rocks to hike, or studying at the university
writing program. Or at Pine Hill where a game's

going on. He might've stayed home,
our singer terrified,

appetite gone, missing some home, pulling
his hair out, tying it into little knots—

don't you know that'll leave you bald,

triggering other ills. The cowboy hat
pool hall glowing like a painting, the elder

outlined in wind, the wind shakes my hand,
the exact tenor, nasal inflection of the Spanish

interpreter defining the terms three languages deep.

We pore over the Treaty of 1868, pages in plastic sheaths,
lit from underneath the glass operating table.

She was young like we all were, but at forty-five, lines
at the corners of her mouth from laughing, from frowning.

Tih timbre tih télii tih táláwosh
we grained, fibered with the hammer end

of a hatchet pulverizing yucca root into soap
ts'ah ts'imshian tl'oh weed can I get some weed
you Alaskans you northern relatives, the sawtooth

Chugach mountains, ghosts, our ghosts?
Sentence elements: subject, verb, the real subject.

Is mastery the gold glint of underpainting
or the black gesso always visible, the internal

shadow, how some humans have animal faces,

wolves often, ravens, too, eyes rendered lovingly,
glint, dab of paint a highlight?

OORT CLOUD

The Twins go searching for arrows, following Lights-up-the-Night among comets and ice songs we've forgotten—just gourd rattle and voice.

The Fair, middle of a water-drummed song, a woman in her best jewelry scowls and says, Quit laughing this isn't supposed to be fun. And you say, I'll show you fun I don't care how old you are, lady.

Later, as you joke with friends the woman says, They must be *drunk* to talk so loud.

A young, slim couple dances skip step—lithe, bouncy style in their moccasined heels. A man in a tall hat and ribbon shirt lights a cigarette, takes a drag and passes it to his friend in matching shirt. Don't worry about her, she's just mean, he says. Golly, Navajos, you say, so impolite.

A circle of cowboys lean over their small drum, crowding the microphone, singing about their search for a Pueblo woman, she was so pretty *heyee yaanaa*. The woman links arms with her Wranglered partner in boots. As she passes she turns her chin and sniffs. You stare at her back and say, Not everything is holy.

Above in the Oort cloud they search for arrows, dodging ice boulders and children of comets while songs are forgotten because even beyond Pluto they can hear ours about the Pueblo woman who came to the dances in Gallup, with long, untied hair and the rest of our lives we've been searching for her.

CORONATION

Smell horses between us. Bring the Fair
dust in your hair, the taste of machined curlyfries.

Atop the Ferris wheel rocking Do not rock the seat.
See all the rides: a child's overturned box of toys.

To the south, rodeo lights, the grounds dusting up—
unbroken, roped horses fresh from the mustang roundup

in the wild horse race. The time the neighborhood strays
got together and killed the tame ones,

pouring yard to yard, weaving through shrubbery
and chain link fencing.

After the horse race, coronation.
Holding hands, stealing through a dust storm, through the powwow
        stands.

Mica streaks chalky on sandstone, on sidewalk.
Every person's pain is their own like measuring a handful of flour.

In spring 1990, we can't park under the shade trees
because of all the broken glass. Inside a truck's metal tank,

you hear footsteps chase you, clanging off the walls.
In the evening, at dinner, you were asked: Frybread or tortilla?

Just before night falls, the carnival lights come on,
The Zipper clangs and shakes, pealing with screams.

At the rodeo grounds the queen gives her acceptance speech
in Navajo. Was that a story about her grandparents? Her dog?

How he howled and howled when they left him.
After the coronation, the Apaches will go out,

marching from the bull gate, led by
their crowned dancers, then women dancers in calico

then lead singer with drum, his backup singers.
And finally you will step down the stands

onto uneven, plowed rodeo ground,
link arms with the arcs of people, and join them.

THE LEAN OF A HORSE'S BODY AT SUNSET

Filing, shaving each corner hooked, each blade, each rung of the chain, each joint, one downstroke after another, sharpening. An angle that would be named in the language, the lean of a horse's shadow at sunset would be the name, with each stroke a name: Long Mustache, Warrior Preparing, SlimYellow Man, Two Faces, Little Singer, Grayboy, Bigwater Man, and the rest.

Everyone agreed that the arrow sticking out of the soldier—between his shoulder blades—was not a Navajo arrow. How could it be? He came from the wrong direction, still tied to his horse. This was lucky. Each file-stroke freeing steel dust, four strokes to a knuckle. Hands, at first greasy with yellow oil, turning black.

The invisible return. Prayed over and killed that Ute in the canyon. Witchcraft. Enemies hired by the Bilagáanas. The Mexican who led them to us had been our captive long ago. Little Mexican, he's called.

This chain will not sharpen no matter how many times I file each tooth. I have to cut, but the motor won't start, so I sit here sharpening. Water trickles, the stream choked by green moss. The women, I want to know, where were the women? Each stroke at an angle. The lean of a horse's body at sunset, its shadow. This wood will not cut itself. Morning. Cold mountain air. First frost already on the ground.

SYNTAX

Split ax, glinting wormwood, Rosẹ's tree, buzz that shakes the ear—
rhododendron before the microphone, Latin from Greek as in *declension*

Please repeat the word, its origin—easiest are the Greek,
large-bodied but harmless, our annual scrimmage against Greyhills

tracing history through language, beloved goods about your neck—
silver, coral, and turquoise, flecks of jet in the eyes of dragonflies

Heuristic: learning the songs without your father; all the god's calls
Nine Nights singing, eating, faint-causing with your fiery voice

A toenail peeling away easy as dead skin—
Vaccination, insemination, branding, long plastic glove

See, this is what's blocking her, my Aunt says,
the calves dropping too early Your uncles didn't time it right—

We're not here to haul your trash, cousin-brother, maternal uncle
hairtie clamped between teeth, learn to make bread—

Construction drags on, cement grows a filament
enjambed in the western hills you'll find green clay

sand will keep mud at bay, the truck unstuck
grin and translate, your blood interpreter, Curly-Headed One,

One Who Missed His Chance, Born With White Hair,
porcupine quills perforate a dog's crying

sage birch oak cottonwood juniper pinon which belong with you?
Who will pay for new teeth? This new syntax is tiresome

Grandchild, a many-bodied train jumbled and torqued
lacerating my lasso. Next time

bring paper and record my biography.

ATOP TÓ ÁDIN MESA

In fly swarms of mosquitos,
foreign wasps, cooped origami cranes
flap their heavy, oiled wings,
a press of maladies: first wind, then malaria,

then all the accusations of thievery
in border town department stores, all the fights
at stoplights, the deaths by exposure.
Still, there are protectors in the pollen:

blue, red, and green, nights when snowstorm
rages dark as the ocean deeps, and hide twangs
inside a cabin, long-stick music, a gloved dance.
In the wood, a grandfather and granddaughter

are confronted by a bear. It rears, snorting, roaring.
Wherefore the man speaks to it, firmly, clearly,
in Navajo: which camp they're going to and why.
Because you must have faith, you must announce your designs.

The snowstorm knocks at the door.
The bear walks away.
We climb stringed light, through corpuscular caves,
broken thoughts and fissured boulders, three sentences

gone wild, winter taking too long to arrive.
Atop Tó Ádin mesa we run,
feet slapping the washboards, breathing fine silt
and girlfriend thoughts, dimpled smiles behind our eyelids,

Three Flowers Brilliantine trickling down our scalps,
and we wish to smell their hands,
the sweat between their breasts.
Listen to their crescendoing laughter.

The Tribal Peacemaker has come, hands clasped
behind her back, thoughts hidden behind whirlwinds
while the boy drinks bleach, while the ankle swells
and purples and our brothers run on without us.

We've been auditioning for a play—
with wigs, with artificial limbs and smiles,
painted-on wrinkles, an eye patch, an imaginary cane.
To those of us who've always shaved our heads I say

Wait, when the man lays out his starched clothes,
wait. Because there is only one size,
and it's too big. There is only one drab color
and it is oppressing.

The Peacemaker watches, still, she listens.
Shaped from mud. For some, the clay
has become brittle. For others it's fired
and tempered with mica—their hearts burn

long and slow, people we warm ourselves to.
Others are still wet, an examining thumbprint
at their lips. Others are sealed with a shiny resin,
a shield, and very few find their way inside.

These are golds, these are emeralds,
this is coral inlaid into the body,
into eyes, eardrums, and whorls.
Stacks of books, infant footprints, wood carvings,

busted bicycles, worn out friends, wool blankets,
pictures hidden inside. Leaves have begun to fall,
but it's still warm, so is it memory?
The transformation: green, yellow-green,

gold, amber, rust; you remember
the annual sorrow. It is good to be sorrowful,
to hear hushed leaves settling, the tick
of stems breaking, wind gusting its percussion.

QUILTING

Four children play WWE in a patch of dirt they've outlined and softened with a spade. But it's still hard and the oldest girl cries when slammed to earth by her little sister.

The fort grows hot this summer, cookie pans warming. Thanksgiving and we miss even the troublemakers, the mean aunties, but most guiltily those who are gone, who, alive, we bore as burdens.

Together we ready our garden, cutting and opening fences, then wait for our uncle with the tractor.

A bomber flies low over the school and everyone—students and teachers and lunch ladies—stops to look up.

A woman weaves and stitches, breaks, picks it up again. For months, crying sometimes. She wipes her face when she comes to the scene of soldiers roping children together by their necks,

Shooting mothers when they try to stop them—some lie bloodied on the ground—the barracks nearby full of chained, raging fathers. They have no faces, but the mothers reach, always reaching, all we can see of fathers are their arms, their hands.

Why remember? Best to forget, they said. But as there are welders and teachers, singers and scientists, so rememberers, too.

Gorman Hall, site of the Navajo Fair Art Show: across from the quilt, a young man sells his comic books. Leaning in when asked about his robots, his superheroes. Why do they look white? I know, he says. I'm trying to change that.

On a cloudy winter day, a father chops wood. The thud reaches us late, long after the blow, bouncing first off the clouds.

EL VOLCÁN

A volcano rises, smoke rumbling, searching
among belching camiones.
Street children drink sugar cane Coke.
Strange condom brands in the tiendas.

The gas man drives by, his tanks in a row,
slowing his troca to yell up ¡El gas!
and blow his horn—a frolicking jingle
that hoots like jungle birds from the south

come to laugh and flash their feathers.
In my small bed I stretch crosswise,
imagine the pines bending in Tsaile.
Missing home and enthralled by

this new one, its own history of violence,
its people darkened as I become in this bright winter.
They say La Malinche betrayed them with her beauty.
That there was a split, a fork between Indian and Future,

between Pueblo and Ciudad, Benito Juárez's time
(himself a good Zapotec Indian),
a "clean slate" quizás, if you will deny,
thinly-veiled or no veil at all, just pact.

Last night women stalked my Black classmates
in the night clubs north of Puebla, Muy exótico.
This morning my hostess's dark house
thick with old lives and small windows—

dark, the anthropologist says,
because they are Aztecan, Mayan.
Diorama: mud and stone, bit of hair.
Look, do you see windows here?

A white beard, a new woman on his arm
when we go out to eat. Baroque
and tiled with talaveras, the De Efe off the plaza.
Statues, flags, roundabout. But I meant

to say something about crossing,
about country and hierarchy, about a bus driver
with a crucifix above his seat.
Every driver, *every* crucifix,
the boys who count the fares.

But ¡El gas! blares outside my window.
The volcano smoldering stares in,
named—say it—El Popo, El Popocatépetl.
And the sun is already up.

CORAL

Woman's choice, this dance. Afterwards, he took his pocketknife and cut from around his neck a string of coral beads. For you, he said, thank you.

The next night he came again; she could tell he was looking for her and couldn't hide his smile when she asked again.

In the end she had enough for a necklace. But he went off with Manycattle to fight them and she never heard from him again.

Strangers warned them. They'd come riding through the mountain, constantly looking back, stopping just long enough to say, They're after us, we've been all the way from Ch'óshgai already.

There were only two horses. They decided that her sister and her niece would take them and she would go on foot. Before they left, hurried, the few sheep running circles in the corral, she gave the many-strand necklace to her niece-daughter. Keep this with the Tó'aheedlíiniis, she said—not saying if I don't come back—and put it over her daughter's head and hugged her.

They went eventually to the canyons and never saw their sister, their little-mother again.

They heard she was captured and imprisoned in the Crying Plain, but they couldn't find her and never knew where she died.

Then my mother gave it to me. Before any others she sought me out. I was between husbands, and she said, I have something for you, it is a responsibility and maybe it will settle you down.

And now I give it to you, niece-daughter, because you show some quality of that woman, making your own decisions, standing up to your uncles. Look how it shines, polished by wear, the color pale, nearly orange. Breathe it, that no one will say it doesn't belong to you.

DO WE STILL POLLEN YOUNG PINES

Do weeds still choke the stream at Black Rock Spring
Is the water still cold
Is the dog unfed tied to a tree
Is it still muddy
Have grasshoppers eaten the field or deer

Do chainsaws still roar
Does the chain still bite
Does Alice shake her can of rocks
Does the old home still stand
Has the mud been blown away
       between the logs to leave it skeleton

Are the cows gone from the stock trailer
       their shit still caked
Does she visit every summer
       our new home with old logs
Does the hummingbird ever get out
Is horny toad still spiked
       in our hands, our throats

Do we threaten They come at night
       and take your hair
Is the house still half-built
Do we still pollen young pines
       praying for height
Do bottles glint with sun
Does mountain lion walk above us

Does the truck still kick up
      a fine silt when we come through with a shovel
Does bread still curl on the grill
Are we still burning our children in the den
Are we still searching for the Twins
Has Reyonda come home or Daryl

Does water still gush from the spring's pipe
Do we still fistfight for water
Does the circle of juniper branches stand from last year
Do we still see her bumping through the woods
Does wind still sound
      thick and roaring through those trees?

AND THE BUTTERFLIES

She will come back in other ways, they said. You'll see her but won't
    know at first, looking out at the sunrise, maybe sunset, maybe
    mountains in winter, a bird as it wings from the woodpile.

I want to say, Please come back, mother. But I can't and don't. It will take
    a long time. Everything will remind you: when the car won't
    start, it will be like your old truck she couldn't start. I saw a
    butterfly today as I ran the trail after work, and knew it was her.
    Crying right there in the middle of my run, tears dripping into
    the dirt.

Everyone used to come for advice: sisters, brothers, even if they'd been
    fighting, broken when a husband left, when their dreams
    wouldn't let them sleep and they feared lightning. She had many
    friends, from her young days to political days to
    prayer woman—they called on her. Strangers drove to her house
    for help, hearing of this strange woman.

She went to Bolivia with her son to teach about rugs. Their medicine
    men in woven hats and bright serapes whispered to each other
    around a fire where they burned coca leaves. We saw you come
    in, what strength you have, like a wave crashing. For a moment
    we were afraid. But she hadn't come to hurt them. She said her
    own prayers to join theirs.

And I was envious of them. All these people taking her time, taking what
    she gave them. But I am your daughter, your first born, your
    Warrior girl, and I miss you. Be patient, she says, you always
    hurry. Now all I have are the sunrises, sunsets, wind through the
    junipers. Butterflies. And they were right.

HEIAU

I have never smelled the rank fur musty smell of bear. Only once in my life have I ridden a horse—in Hawaii on the north shore where a small sunburnt lady settled her four-horse corral. If Eddie stops to eat on the trail, she hollered, it's because he's forgotten you're on his back—in all that leafy greenness thick coily roots and reedy trunks turning sharp ridges velvet the smells rich with old earth overripe like the mangoes that fell in our driveway in August oozing into dark red soil and the world of ants. What a horse I whisper shilíí' I'm still here and he never steps off the trail. Shilíí' hazlíí'—my horse has appeared, has come into being. We saunter clopping to where a hill of lava rocks rises jagged with air holes air of people we will never know a silence inside silence the sea horizon blue. In their Honolulu apartments the whitewash gone yellow and outside on balconies their yellowing surfboards rusted bicycles their cars crackling in the sun and I think of my own car fading in my desert the paint flecking away until it is a skeleton whispering for another ride.

Deer this morning beside the road big ears skinny head bent low to the shoots of green sprung up around what once was Red Lake now a green and yellow field of weeds the deer calling plunge your heads into the willows choking the stream. Bįįh means *deer* but what did it mean before the Apaches split from us to live in teepees and sing water drum songs, dance arm in arm. Still we talk in our language because we know they'll understand. The old Hawaiians carried all those rocks Heiau and watched them for movement remembering their own journey across the ocean. A woman gets up to sing in the thick morning air full of flower horse sweet rot and far away coming high on the wind the salty smell of ocean opening over the rocks the trade winds. Time to push boat into bay into surf beyond whitecaps flaring the horizon ripples and far away visible just below the clouds the ghost of an island.

IT'S TIME TO PUT THE WILD MUSTANGS TO SLEEP

One summer we plucked cicadas
from their field of din, removed their limbs,
seventeen years growing, rolled them in pale cornmeal.
Years later I found their husks still clinging
to rusted nails, rabbit's foot, and snakeweed.
That summer's music was their pervasive
static, the mealy crunch between our ears.

A killer whale leaps from the ocean,
surprising tourists in their ferry,
the northern Pacific where spruce trees pull mountains
from water. I was a journalist and everyone
wanted me to write their story, the handicapped
and able-bodied both.

In the movie a woman cries
through labor, screaming
sweat pouring down her face.
What advice for your young man?
Strength runs through blood like horses.
The years go by slowly but then you wake
and they've disappeared like ties on a railroad track.
Be a bitch, no more sweet girl says yes to everything.

My sister lets her dog run
at Frenchy's Park and a woman
jumps sputtering into her face—
We've been trying to return these prairie dogs
to their natural habitat, she shouts,
It's been going so well,

choking back tears,
Who do you think you are, the Queen of Frenchy's?

The Jemez Mountains with their aspens,
white cliffs, summer fire.
You haven't changed, the ex says,
the glass sweating in her hand.
I'm trying to, trying to.
A tornado touches down that same summer
on Many Farms Mesa. I saw it, says the witness,
tunneling for me, nowhere to run out there.

College students dance in a fraternity basement
fogging windows, hoping to touch,
to go home with someone but what is home there
among the viny brick and endless rolling hills?

It's time to put the wild mustangs to sleep.
They've eaten the grass, scoured
what was left from overgrazing.
We have a soft spot for horses
shaking their manes like pine shakes wind,
symbol of power, of history.
Tongues longer than cows' they grasp plants by their roots
and rip the land apart. Herds careen the plain.

Put the mustangs to sleep.
The world splits like a flood
around a tree, glass to coal and coal
to whatever's left.

Cicadas burrow through the field, their husks
old lives we've left behind
shivering in wind when we remember them.

PERFUME I

Our scent issues from our scalp, under our arms, between our legs. We
    all know, all hunt for it—even when perfume is sprayed, or
    lotion rubbed into skin—like searching out a melody
    among the static of twenty radios. The moon plays back our
    cries. The pleasure—

The wake: Everyone assembled in the same house, the same room,
    missing, aching, huddled in grief. In Mexico they make skulls
    out of candy. Are they hard or soft? Sweet or stale? Raisins.
    Raisins are enough for the ceremonial cake. Oversweet and
    you'll go on wanting, wishing after someone more. After their
    sweet and bitter smell. The way they comb or do not comb.
    Brush and stroke. Clip.

A pair of glasses that turn dark blue in the sun, leave a clear thumb hole
    if that's how you hold them. I distracted myself with them at
    the memorial. The yellow raspberries fell off the stems whenbarely
    I touched them, the last good ones, the rest overripe and orange,
    eating themselves. Tasting like honey. Harvest time, and the
    pumpkins turn yellow out of green.

In northern Oregon it rains lightly but often, cloudy many days,
    especially autumn and winter, so wool is fine. Here we
    have storms, the looming, the smell turning thick and rich, the
    sheets when it lands, releasing our pent up anger, unmistaken.
    get caught—you'll get cold. Don't wear a hat—you'll scare off
    the clouds.

A motorcycle slips and skids, leaving a long, swerving track in the mud.
    Squeeze it between your fingers. Rummaging through the
    weeds, rolling in them, finding a broken-winged bird. That's
    enough. Hey, shake out these blankets before the moths get them.

HALLOWEEN

This Halloween we party in the mountains,
in the piney wood behind an old Spanish church
from the days of frays and The Requirement.
Arrayed like toys in our costumes we drink
and dance to electronic music, lights strung
between ponderous branches
flashing with the bass. An elm's leaves fallen,
nearly November, a Friday this year—

Greasewood pops like fat.
Two werewolves and Wonder Woman have started a fire,
warming hands and asses—

My friend the photographer jumps around
waving his disembodied head,
jaw-length hair flying—

De Vaca and Estéban marched here with Aztecs
and Xlaxcalans to strongarm,
to cut arms, to garrote—

My friend dances, the music gallops,
the lights match. Past Taos they met
Kiowas where they garroted
their Kiowa interpreter.
He'd told them of gold cities.

Garrote: piece of wire, cable, cord,
also an iron collar that when looped
about a person's neck can be twisted
and tightened, closing the windpipe,

breaking skin, tearing, cinching
to the spine, and finally, severing—

A high voice calls us: Dance all night,
dance all night, remix these costumes,
werewolf, Wonder Woman, man with no head,
trade until we can't tell which is which,
who is who. Are you lover or ex-lover?
Are you friend or foe?

THE ASTRONOMER

A garbage man lifts a bin to shake trash into his truck, but it's packed too tight, so he slams the aluminum bin over and over onto the lawn, spewing trash until it's empty. Then he throws the entire battered can into the truck's open mouth.

Snow collects on the quad—half a foot, a foot, nearly two. Streetlights blink on in the early night lending our faces an orange glow, snowflakes on our eyebrows.

On La Bajada hilltop someone lies on the ground between the freeways, their sedan on its side. People kneel or stand—no ambulance yet. The man who caused the accident steps out of his car where it's skidded off the road after veering into oncoming traffic, staggers, waves his hands, palms up: It wasn't me. All gilded with an orange, glowing sunset, a purple thunderstorm curtains the east.

In this version we still practice our penmanship in Big Chief tablets, marking an even line, trying not to tear a hole in the thin gray paper. Dick and Jane are stranded on the island with night coming. All yellow has disappeared from the book.

In this version the silos at Fort Wingate still carry missiles in their wombs.

Eclipse emerges and we go inside, listen to the quiet of birds, even crows gone silent.

We wake and the astronomer stares stunned at the stars; he had shot them from his cannon earlier that night, spraying them everywhere. We find him reaching, leaping, crying,
trying to bring them back in.

TUBA CITY

I.

The coach paces the sidelines, shouting at his opponents, stomping when
      they shoot, longing to be in the game, to have the ball in
      his hands, to make decisions, to win games—to lose them would
      be better than this.

The snowboarder stops at the lip of the half pipe alongside his friend.
      Who's going first? I'm not going first. Somebody's gotta go first.

Sitting boldly on the adobe wall, the black cat swipes at passersby.

Under a full moon we ski the Valles Caldera—four pairs of tracks in
      snow. When we get to a hill, only two of us go up, the snow so
      bright we can see clear across to the first line of trees.

One of the extra credit questions is: Who is Tuba City named after? C.)
      Toova, a Hopi chief.

Take this juniper ash for your bad dream. To make more, burn the
      branches, gathering what's left into a foil envelope.

The Paiutes have descended the mountain to live with us again. The girls
      herd sheep with us.

The telephone poles have been transformed, snow hooding the ceramic
      and glass fixtures.

Rock-with-Wings is from a longer name, one that recalls the monster f
      lying the sky above, alive.

II.

After summer rain, a motorcycle tears up Buffalo Pass, two teenagers
       astride. The girl at the handlebars, the boy clinging to her waist.

While the cement is fresh, the logs are old, felled and stripped seventy
       years ago. But still good, still bearing the ax tooth.

A volleyball player dives under the shorebreak at Sandy Beach as he's
       done countless times to feel the wave tearing at his trunks, legs,
       ankles. But this time he's a moment too slow, and the heavy,
       crashing lip catches his shoulders and slams his head into the
       sand. The ocean throws him, a jumble of limbs, onto the wet
       sand, and people rush to him as the water tugs them back and
       another wave looms.

Still, they fly kites on the grass field near the parking lot. Still, the east
       wind catches the dark hair of women drying off as his friends
       drag him, limp, up the shore, lay him on the beach, and begin CPR.

After five years of everyday wear, the inlay buckle is chipped at one
       corner, shiny yellow shell arranged herringbone. A gift from
       the new wife to replace the buckle from the old. The poet says,
       It's been around the world and back.

The summer is young, but inside the cabin the cement floor is cool and
       we plaster between logs with our chinking guns and sleep on the
       floor, sometimes hearing the huffing of black bears.

JUNGLY

The doorway full of whispers this morning,
the camber of drying ceremonial cake,
of concomitant day-after blues,
silence from the elderly comandante
whose march we'd followed all through the weekend,
because a Blessing awaited at the end.

The sunbeam is slender, the westcoast brimming
with roiling waves, the dogs are shitting on my lawn,
a murder of scarecrows surrounds my elm tree.

You miss your old voice—
softer, higher, no hard edge frosting your words.

The man with no legs says It took me five years
to stop remembering.

Ask, I tell my friend. Ask what you're fighting for!
I want to shake him. But really I want to shake myself.
Verb for grabbing your own shoulders.

As the cantaloupe slides down your throat,
a woman dips a clay jug into the spring
and a cornered fox lunges and snaps.
That's why sky like lichen, blue like greenery,
unseen stream, cow carcass strung from a tripod hoist,
your garden went all jungly.

Rafters parallel into an A-frame,
the skeleton visible as one
lies on the floor looking up, easy to see

the policies from here, to wend a way.
On one side is language, prickly, standing up;
on the other an unfinished sidewalk.

I'll bring you home to my parents.
They can be reasonable, you'll see.
At the dam, hundreds of frogs wail the night.
I tell my friend, my eldest brother,
the green fires are actually blue.
The comandante has summoned you,
me, and the interpreter. The rainstorm flowers,
then casts lightning. A red-tipped fox trots lazily out.
The knives adjust themselves in the dishwasher.
The fight passes over us.

DRY WHITE PLAIN

If they killed my mother, my brother, like anyone—revenge. And you?
Stories of a dangerous chaos, the Long Walk, the land sprouting with Utes,
Kiis'áanii, whites, even enemy Navajo stealing sheep and cattle—

Gut shot, a man flees on his horse from whites near Salt Lake. Gunshot after
gunshot he hears his three friends executed. He sings for them when night
falls—but what to bury when the enemy has taken their bodies?

Composing songs, framing the night sky through a hogan smoke hole,
carrying them with his frosted breath. I have seen old men cry who weren't
there, who heard a grandmother tell them the story—

Drought after drought, still up to our necks in it we trod the dry ground,
our terrible dust cloud, steeling of heart and guts—

Deelté, warrior training on horseback, hiding in canyons, among cliffs,
waiting for hooves, for shouts in English or warning from the cliff tops.
Driven to Wailing or Halgai Hatéél—Dry White Plain in the east—
Kiowa land.

Or forced to live smashed together like the Hopis. So we revenge on white
men, women, and children for taking ours. Which become captives, which
do we kill?

Drinking boiled sagebrush to empty his gut shot intestine, applying
a poultice to stay alive through snowy nights and in his delirium
journey home.

Thus our games today in St. Johns, Cortez, Durango, Farmington, Flagstaff
are angry, recalling with young muscles, shouts for the ball—

Take out that boy, no mercy, no rules. Only skin, bone, blood, flushed faces, us and them, yours or mine because a massacre happened—

Many before and after, but this one we remember our relatives died fleeing. The crowd roars—

But wait. Look through the smoke hole framing the night, winter sky, stars appearing—

Go on grazing, horses, let me watch from here. No windows in this house yet, sighing one by one—

The stars cool and cool our breath like snow. Nothing, no lamenting, no more wincing, but joining the cold light, the odd gentling of pines inside.

TRIBES

They play dirty, says the viejo from Escalante,
his lower lip jutting out, shaking his head.
Did you see them yelling at the refs?
The game is tight, the boys lithe, glistening,
sweat shining off the contours of biceps,
Laguna-Acoma in blue against the small-town boys
like it has been since you can remember.
The LA coach, a bald chihuahua of a man,
has drilled into them elasticity, so they press,
pass and run the break, see patterns appearing.
The orange Raiders are themselves balanced
by a heady point guard and attacking wings,
but in the fourth quarter LA breaks the game open.
The Pueblo boys see the passing lanes unfold
and sail the ball past the orange jerseys.
Their blue defense is everywhere, sneakers squeaking,
trapping the corners, the coach a mirror
on the sideline, squatting with his hands out,
hopping when they make a steal, pumping his fists.
When the Raiders call time,
the Hawks run to each other smiling, high-fiving,
and the blue-shirted crowd roars, shaking
plastic clappers and pom-poms so when the orange
fans across the court stand up—the men in camo
and cowboy hats, the moms holding signs—to begin
their Go Raiders cheer, the blue crowd raises
its deafening L-A-Ha-awks and drowns them—
heads thrown back, shouting, shaking fists,
tribes again. I remember this acid taste.
I remember why I don't like you.
This burning-wood smell. So the blue yell buries.

Angrily, the tallest cowboy fan sweeps his arm,
then slumps into his seat. They can't hear themselves
anymore. The rest of the orange fans sit, too,
until there is only one woman standing.
She holds *Go Raiders Go* above her head,
waves it and howls, takes a breath
and howls again.

On the court the players are trying
to beat each other to the ball. Boys
who practice their jump shots in supermarket lines
waiting for their mothers, in diners along the interstate
going east to west a tournament that will
hold them high on its hardwood shoulders
above cheering girls and red scoreboard bulbs.
They walk through the snow and mud of the pueblo,
sneakers tied across the backs of their necks.
The pressure is on but we can still get a good shot.

The Escalante fan waiting for the next game
when his team will play, red polo shirt,
white crew cut, switching from English to Spanish,
points his chin at the blue crowd, Pendejos,
shakes his head and glares, brow furrowing
because though this isn't his team,
he knows his side. Now you get angry
and say, That's right, they beat
those cowboys, killed them in that last
quarter did you see that? Because you are sitting
in their section. A few people turn around
to stare; you glare back. But the blue roar rises,
drowning you out, too. The last buzzer sounds,
the orange boys cover their faces with towels,
slump into folding chairs, heads in hands

because these were the semis.
The other bench empties, boys leap
and hug teammates, yell to the rafters,
raise their arms to the fans: Louder.
Tomorrow they play for the title,
for the championship, versus the private school,
the always champs, the Christians.

SWEET JUICE

They have cut all the juniper branches
for Nidáá' tonight, have fanned them
on the ground, built a brief house
for the ceremony—a ponderosa sliced into slats,
blue tarp for the door. But this morning it's empty,
everything eerie until Grandmother drives up
in her pickup. Having a good run?
She swings her arms like a runner.
Stay, she says, for the singing.

But I don't. We keep things after they're spent:
packaging for a drill whose functions we already know,
the cardboard box that earrings came in.
After you hit your head you seemed fine,
remembered where you were, your name
and mother, your job on Monday. But then
you forgot to turn on car lights,
jumped violently when someone knocked,
snapped when your niece
spilled Coke on your couch.

Though you have filled a feeder with sweet juice,
there are no hummingbirds.
Though it's October—year's backbone—
there is no cold, and leaves cling resolutely
to branches. In Dinétah she made it rain,
standing on a bridge, praying over Navajo Dam.
The sky turned gray, clouds thundered over
and dropped male rain.
See, she said, they hear us.

THE HOUSE AT LONG CORNFIELD

We skirt mesas in Hopi land, view sandy plains, blue valleys and distant San Francisco Peaks, short houses hanging off cliff's edge—Shungopavi, Oraibi, then down into fields, Moenkopi. Minds in the mood for travel, returning to red, to blue trees cottoning. A white dog sits on the shoulder, head laid on paws until we pass, traffic on a Saturday.

I believe they helped us plant corn. And, neighboring, we visited their medicine men, their language like water running down sandstone. Route 66, Interstate 40, were dirt roads winding up the mesa. Even the trails to Fort Sumner that became billboards flaking in fifty years of sun.

We race with them first as children, now as men and women up mesas, down arroyos, kicking rocks, leaping cacti. After this summer's race in honor of Tewanima, Hopi Olympian, I hunched over, hands on my knees. The stone steps we'd climbed in the last mile took everything, the people hanging over the edge shouting in water language. I gulped mouthfuls from a plastic bottle then splashed the rest on my face until water ran into the dirt, where it pooled before sinking. A boy with a braid let go of his father's hand, ran up and kicked dirt on my feet, then glared at me. In front, his hair was cut into fringe. As the announcer called the winners, I realized he'd covered the water. His dad, with the same hairstyle, laughed at us both.

This was before we drove back through Chilchinbeto, changed, before we stopped in Kayenta and you talked with a grandmother who spoke only Navajo, who scolded us for joining too soon after the ceremony—we couldn't sit on the same bed in her house. Still, she called me Son when we said goodbye. This was before we got stuck in Many Farms' purple clay, before we sat in an old hogan between Black Mesa and Navajo Mountain where people used to camp among junipers and orange sand on their way to Kayenta or Tónaneesdizí or a Nine Night Sing. A place called Dá'ák'eh Haneezí—Long Cornfield. That field is gone now, but some people still name it, touching the age-old, the time-worn.

There was another dog beside the road in Hopi, bent at its work, clamping and pulling. It looked up as we drove by, then turned back to what lay there—carcass of another dog. We passed into their land of flat-roofed houses, netless basketball hoops, and there, standing alone, were four poles, wire fencing falling away—the remains of a backstop. And though it was empty, they must still play, tossing the ball, runners on base, crack of a bat, fans honking their horns flashing their lights—but for us it was empty and January then, the last snowfall not yet melted when we drove through on our way, though we didn't know it yet, to the house at Long Cornfield.

CALMER DAYS

Stories are about us and people: are we really a people?—

He carries the rainbow on his back, emblazoned with stars, shot through
with incendiaries, imagining the sharp bones under a face—

The critique has shut you down, laid low your villi like years of
smoking—

The muscle atrophies, hunger after anger because anger slips away like
water through rocks—

In spring the winds arrive early, whipping over snow, tasting our hair, our
faces smelling of wind when we come inside—

The willows withhold scent, waiting for calmer days—

FOUR DOGS

You wake to the plain cut by early stars. First you must remove the dogs, four of them skittering around the shed and juniper trees. Call them, hold your hand out and pick them up under their muscular bellies, hoist each into the pickup bed where their claws clack, until they stand looking at you warily, ears up, dipping their shoulders. Collarless, fit from running, hunting, following horses, trained to be called to a stop when they see sheep. Though he omits the possessive, they are the boy's dogs.

The boy who'd been riding that day with his cousin the young bullrider with the quick smile and stutter. They had been roping and riding the neighbor's cows. Their boots caked with drying mud. The dogs will stay while you enter the hogan for the final sing, last one before sunrise, before gray and then blue-lighted stars. Your in-laws told you, The dogs are running around, and you understood why it was important you do this small duty during an intricate ceremony. Water, charcoal, ash. If you can find young bullriders who still help.

Night: first, stars prick the curtain, then swimming dark and dogs go quiet—who can recall them from deep night? Finally last quiet, last silence before birds return from the north. The singing picks up even as you tire, grey morning rolling through the doorway, where the blankets have been pulled back, the dogs beside the truck now, waiting. We walk without jackets to the plowed ground, there to dump the water.

SINGING TREES

Yishwoł: to be running along
to have designs on it
to run pawing at your ankle
run with shoes untied
run after a woman
chase turkeys into a tree
to face westward, backwards at sunrise
to whistle, to blow a bone flute
to bore holes in the ice, to bore holes
into the skull where water bubbles up
cold and sticky, rises about your galoshes
to round up your words with a whip
the donkeys braying
to ascend the fault line
just past the windmill
dead cows on your left
to corner the messenger
graze her ears at the point
where we frighten our children
with our yelling, our smashed dishware
because the message lives inside us
dormant until called forth by some argument
or strand of hair or lotion scent.
Keep animals, fight dogs
reach into your pocket for husks
assist in laying the cake—

To hear your questions, jet-black
the road invisible as we round the turn
to red horses, our car collapsing
green across our side windows, the odor thick

in whiskey creek where a clan became human
walked across the mountain pass
and met their relatives among green rocks
the creek full from winter sunlight
dwindling like hope until they saw smoke
and heard a man singing full and loud
holding his grandson's hand
when he came out of the trees
saw them and stopped—

ELECTION DAY

He was wrapped in politics,
right hand man to the administration,
while she was caring for four children.
T'óó bił tł'éé'. To be filled with night.
Someone else has written about
darkness, the night-darkness you can't see,
a curtain over your eyes as though it were night.
Fields flattened, corn stalks eaten by deer,
teeth marks on those still standing.

At the chapter house:
the gilded man.
Silver necklace, heavy bracelets,
stones hanging from his ears.
She should have married this man,
dressed for the dance tonight.
Her husband would never dress like that.
Love your children and hate your husband—
that's easy. She smells the office on him
as though he's popped out of Tupperware,
hair slicked back and shiny this morning,
cigarettes and perfume.
Is it wrong?
To see her husband in her son's smile and say,
Stop that, you look like him.

Bare shoulder in moonlight,
jay in the morning,
windshield cracks on an old Chevy
rusting under the cottonwood,
toolshed filled with mouse droppings,

then cat droppings,
paw marks on the dirt,
baling wire to latch the door.
I voted today, she tells him,
at the chapter house.
She saw her there. The woman smiled at her
like nothing was wrong
until she told her I know.

I know, you bastard, I know.
His face went stony and he stayed outside
fiddling in the shed until night.

She wears that sticker like a badge all next day,
red, white, and blue,
little stars around the edge:
I Voted Today.
She piles his things into the old Chevy,
first in back, then fills
the cab with leftover pants and shirts.

It sits there until his new car
rolls down the long dirt drive.
She calls her children:
Come here, babies.
It's time to say goodbye to your dad.
He's going away.

FROM WHEATFIELDS TO WHISKEY CREEK

Stars recede when ranch lights flicker on—an airplane runway to Round Rock. We are not alone. Out to Wheatfields and catch some fish. I stripped down to underwear and jumped in at Whiskey Creek, whose real name I never knew. My cousins joined me because it's always too crowded at Wheatfields, especially since the ranchers have taken to gouging muddy ruts with their big trucks. Who were your best friends but your cousins? It wasn't a lake until the government dammed the north end where Black Rock rises among woolly pines. Every other year, the trucks back down the concrete ramp, open their bellies and out come fish, tiny young trout splashing into water. People drown, every once in a while you read it in the paper, if not there then your auntie or uncle will say they fell off their boat in the middle. Eight feet deep and they couldn't swim. Come now, away from there, let the fishermen have their new sport. Dry off and we'll get on the road from Whiskey Creek.

NEED

n the white-hot nape of summer,
where redwing finches hang
from lengths of string,
at an intersection a mile from your home,
you climbed out of this world,
out of a burning wreck,
two cars at an intersection,
and, walking away, realized
your grandmother was still inside.
How to find empathy
when only brake lights are left burning?
The blank look on your lover's face
when you tell him, Nothing left.
You hear the crackling in a chest
where the world is made whole again
in a gust of mountain air.
The first time you hear eagles
is not in flight, but on an Alaskan beach
where dozens, perhaps hundreds
feed on fish stranded in the shoals,
and they are not crying
like in the movies, but whistling—
in an instant you understand how
the whistle blown over a powwow drum
gets its name—
at that beach of wings, white caps
and fishermen tying boats from the sea.
This summer of storms—
Buffeted in the high desert
after the driest year ever.
This should be your respite. But

the traffic outside knots
your intestine, quipu, to make agreement,
to send messages of war
but for you they signal effort,
labor, and infinite pages ahead.

A couple dances on the plaza,
the last concert of summer,
rhinestones on her jean pockets,
swinging each other as tourists
tap their feet. They are childless.
She's slim and lithe, an instructor
of yoga and therapeutic massage.
The bald man wears a dark shirt,
a smile. They love like brushfires
that become forest fires and devour
the neighboring mountains.
They simmer and burn love to ash.
Is it worth it to struggle
when we've hardened, to crack
open our brittle shells? How far
goes the gorge, our Rio Grande?
How deep in the churned-up earth?
Not recognizing your own smooth faces
in a fifteen year-old photo.

A high mountain field,
easy to see the valley, where you refuged
from blue-coated enemies.
An old shelter still there
at the field's crest, just above
cattle now grazing,
a triangle of logs that sinks lower
and lower each year,

eventually to lie flat— spokes of a wheel.
This thrum when you see me,
seized by smell, furious
in your need and startled by mine.

TWO-BY-FOUR

In the middle of night, a few hours before trucks rumble through and empty trashcans into their bellies, we see hungry brothers picking through them.

Limp and unbreathing when I picked it up, the kitten had been killed by another cat. Life, they say. If I imagine playing in a creek as a boy in my underwear, you will say first you learn sight, then laughter, and finally how to walk upright, search for food and other people's laughter.

Swimming is something I cannot teach. Instead I throw my friends in the pool and jump in after. When is an explosion orderly? One day the editor came in and told his staff, Someone keyed my car yesterday. Do they think that will keep us from making the news? They can chop off my hands and I'll type with my goddamn feet. We were proud of his bravado in our small newsroom nation.

That's what it takes when semis leave their dome lights on, when the government sends its hitmen. We have been downsized, crammed into little rooms, represented by little men with big mouths. Outside the Council Chambers, protests continue, signs weave in the wind. And then maybe word reaches us that the shooting has stopped, there was only one gun, and it's time to throw our two-by-fours onto the woodpile.

SWEAT

Do we believe our mothers when they tell us, The water will not
       hurt you? Do we miss our fathers when they don't post our bail?
       A windmill creaks in summer, stands still in winter, snow frosting
       its blades.

Morning and we are off to work. Coffee in our holders, hay flying off the
       trailer in front of us like dandruff. Graffiti streaks across the
       corrugated walls of the empty mill, pink outlined in electric blue.
       Rained early so the quickened earth breathes into our open
       windows, the sagebrush combusting and torn open. If we have
       lost our son, we bring his shoe to our face and breathe his last sweat.

The orange rock faces glisten and cry, sunlight cracking over their
       heads. Just before the stoplight in town, two dogs run headlong
       from 7/11 to Fina and we brake slightly. We are workers
       on the hill, in big box houses, old stone buildings, layer
       cake offices, government departments, resting our hands, palms
       up, on stacks of paper.

Lunch at the Mexican restaurant and a twin-engine jet falls from the
       sky to land in someone's old cornfield between the rocks. Our
       families evolve, our daughters grow breasts and move out, and
       only a clan reunion once every five years will bring them back to
       play childhood games, race with eggs held in plastic spoons,
       family tree displayed prominently under the big
       cottonwood, its branches hand drawn, the lettering steady
       and neat.

PERFUME II

How could anyone love you? I said. Enough to leave their wife, their
longtime partner. Eight days later I came upon gray ice at a frozen
beach, breathed cold moist air, the last third of winter.

How a coat becomes a second skin. You know all the pockets, your own
smell trapped in the lining. The tribal judge tells a story: After
death, the lover smells what hangs in her husband's closet. Not
washing, not giving away, not letting go. Now what does that
tell you? She also claims to be a medicine woman, but we're right
to be skeptical.

Watching their sons play, the mothers are overjoyed, elated that the boys
understand their different dialects, and so dinner is a warm affair,
toys everywhere, action figures on the table, salmon and rice—we
have become People.

We left our children home alone to grind corn while we visited
relatives—and they were safe.

Looking up the trail, the mountain lion resembles a dark dog, but its
shoulders and footfalls are new designs.

Our discussion has led to a quarrel: who will do the cleaning? who
will do the bleaching? The sun falling behind us turning the
sky orange.

The mountain lion has vanished. Deer graze the same spot, leaping low
pines when we startle them.

BACKBONE

The stream turns brown and birds go quiet, then, like irrigation into
      a field, the river turns, a yellow blanket thrown across from bank
      to bank. The Chairman holds the murky water in a clear mug,
      examines it in sunlight, then kneels and dips again, as though
      trying to catch something.

A stinkbug crosses the road, the sun shining purply off its back, flips
      when a car whooshes over it.

The wild turkeys of autumn flap their way into a Ponderosa, shedding
      feathers, but without calling. A bobcat runs at the edge of
      headlights along the gravel road, then veers and leaps onto a
      cottonwood stump and watches the truck rumble by.

The line at a food stand backs up and up, disrupting oncoming traffic at
      the flea market, and people get angry. What's the holdup?
      someone says. They ran out of sheep intestine, so they
      sent somebody to the store.

The tribal college president walks through the cubicles, sees a woman
      whispering to her friend and thinks everyone is out to get her,
      all these small, rude people, shooting her down.

They were grooming me to be a leader, he tells his son, and I
      disappointed all of them. But hey, I still rodeo.

A truck whistles weightless over the washboards, rain ignites the
      sagebrush field, the watermelon huge in the yard, on their way to
      have a say on the fences.

A backbone, my backbone, the ripple in sandstone.

WHEN ANIMALS USED TO TALK

1.

These are the lungs, the knuckles, the fingernails (one gone black),
     beside it the foot, beside that the heart and blood systems—
     different between man and woman, as is the talk behind
     closed doors.
This is the brain after a bike accident, after growing up with your
     mother's sister, after growing up in a boarding school. Wary of
     the cliff dwelling.
These are the rocks from the buffalo drive, the long chute. One leg lifted
     up in tai chi every day at seven a.m. Blood memory. When
     animals used to talk.
She shouted like the bear could understand her. I thought she must
     be going crazy. But if you are steadfast within, if you have
     rubbed the grease from your lips, then ask the bear permission
     to pass through.
On the trail we lie down and listen. First crickets return, then the avian
     twitter, then a fly thrums our ear. Finally we've been still long
     enough to recognize the wind bending through piñon pine.

2.

In Japan, a tsunami. Water swallows an entire city. Five years later, a son
   calls his father (missing, presumed dead) from a phone booth.
   He was on a delivery to the city when the tsunami hit. Why did
   you make me different by dying? I wish you would come back. I
   want to talk to you again, dear Dad.
Another man steps into the booth and calls his family. Where are you?
   I'm so sorry I couldn't save you. I'm all alone without you,
   daughters, son, wife-mother. I'm so lonely. I'm so lonely.
And you, what would you say in the telephone booth?
   Would you accuse? Reminisce into the receiver? Or not say a
   word and cry for the first time in five years?
I would say, Forgive me, I was just a boy. I would say, Who do I turn to?
   Who will teach me? I am a man now, and all your cautions were right.
The waves lap the shore, languid, but never tired. We have been
   gambling, but now it's over. In this way night becomes day; in
   this way a log opens and giants tumble out.

CARSON CITY, 1957

Pale yellow walls trellis around the sink mirror she eases the door closed slumps to the tiled floor. Breathe breathe breathe the children out playing and yelling. Crying pricked by the tacks holding carpet to kitchen floor her shoulder against the door. The asphalt cicada din presses around her mountains bursting highway heaving up neighbors waving in the sun smiles chiseled into their faces eyebrows sewn on with a broken machine. Their clothes flowered socks blue topstitching on a man's trousers but she can't see their heads for the glare. She blinks and the sun jumps overhead here where mountains descend and cacti burst from the cracked ground. Water water water. The cars snake tracks in the dirt the vinyl interior inflates pressing into her face. The felt tacking on the roof sags and wraps around her tongue. Who will save her at the house? The man at work going deaf in a blue hole jackhammering a new bank casino warehouse. Carries the machine wail home in his mouth. No. The children cry heaving sobs and her face crumbles. Catches it in the trellis mirror the lines around her mouth and red brick. She was a majorette. The wall lists to the right lists until the ceiling flips. Say it. The walls swallow. *Say* it. Citrus smell of shiver and sweat. *She came over the mountain singing sing sing* she wraps her arms around herself tucks her dress under. *She looked out over the prairie dogs the crying prairie dogs the wind bending the yucca fruit low.*

NOW THE REVOLUTION

A man hitches to the football stadium to watch his son. Weaves his way through the fans to sit beside his wife. Don't say anything, she hisses, I don't want to hear any of it. Elbows on knees, he looks down at his shoes, swaying.

If we were our own country there would be many revolutions, maybe as many as Mexico. Two would be dictatorial, following a man full of charisma whose fist came through the radio, who sealed borders, created a national language, a national bird, nationalism. Windows would be tinted with our golden flag, the Sawmill revived, ambassador to America dressed in slab earrings, blazer and cowboy boots. The vestiges of departments and divisions, cubicles still plastered with photographs, many new hogan-shaped hangars for business—bonfires in the middle, a vision of the home, but expanded. Always a problem with ventilation, though. Shorthand for computer: thinker. Shorthand for chairman: twisting head.

Raking wind, rumbling traffic, car rending freshly wet highway, signal lights blinking, sagebrush scent. The hitchhiker is you, the duffle bag yours, walking past Haunted Canyon. How to wake a dead computer: pour tea into a mug and wait. The new punk rockers wail in Gorman Hall while the C-W dance thumps along next door in Nakai. Both halls dark, but the punk band has blinking lights above their drummer. Boots scuff and slide—you must decide whether to muss your hair or don your hat. A strobing glimpse of the lead singer, teeth flashing, T-shirt ripped, leaning through his hair. And now the ringing. Now the revolution. Now the silence in your ears.

RED MESA

Chris Jackson's gotta shake his arm after two dribbles at the freethrow
line. He's gotta twitch an ankle, gotta bring knee to chest after
sinking the long shot, blink twice and catch himself. Missing from
the deck, mother would never let you stay this long slamming doors,
messing up.

Shopping cart outside my house from the dollar store, its rear grate
twisted up over the handlebars—did you bring it here? Why do
snowshoes keep you up? Why did grandma sell the best jewelry, the
ones she's supposed to've saved for me?

The Tilt-a-Whirl at the fair made me barf so go ahead, catch you at the
Hammer. And don't wait up, the powwow won't get better,
midnight's gone, the Special done, all that's left, Jingle Dress. Buy me
a drink baby and I'll walk you home, too late to be here alone.

Watch out for your scalp, they like to get down in there and dig it out.
Where's the trash bucket? Don't know now that grandma kicked
us out. You keep Jayden—I've got class today. And get a job, CD,
there's a new boss since your fight with the tire man. Might have to
be a Wednesday wash, buckets are nearly empty.

To shake your man gotta break your rhythm, come down and pop-pop,
two quick ones so he's leaning, all you need, got him beat. Practice,
practice, practice. Don't need too much skill, just a little bit.

They say they killed them all in that cave and we found them later
walking through our dreams, going in and out like Beaver coming up
for air, a piece of wood in his mouth to give to us.

And that's Spider Rock, where She lives. Bring your pollen and pray,
every time. You're from Red Mesa? So am I, but I don't think it's

the one you're talking about. Don't mind them, you'll find those people wherever you go. They're hungry. We have all kinds: rich and poor, strong and weak. Take care of your car. Keep it running, don't give up. Carry this and say it loud so the wind can hear you.

LIFT YOU LIKE A LAMB

Chisel lines radiate from the buckle's center, the scribe marks polished until mere dots now, the bail cutout a window. Inside we see a fair—no rides this time. The people dressed in best clothes, best jewelry, best shoes. A government recruiter sets up in Gorman Hall with bright pictures of Detroit, Chicago, Los Angeles. Smiling men in hard hats and gloves, sharing I-beams, on their way to build skyscrapers. In pressed shirt and pleated trousers the recruiter waves, beckons, his hair short as a dog's. Over the hill they hear dances, but say We'll camp this side.

A family gathers for dinner outside the hogan to see summer's last sunset. Potatoes and ground beef still warm in coals from the dying fire. Descending from the clouds: a slender, ripening air.

A singer comes home to a man's footprints on his threshold, the threshold that he had swept clean that morning before his rounds. He decides not to question his wife, the whole thing shameful now.

A girl brings in the sheep and closes the corral's gate, knowing she will leave for school tomorrow. She will miss the kid goats, how they play, butt heads, for her entertainment it seems, in the shallow canyon. How they shake their heads when she scolds them playfully.

Even though he is dying and scared, the old man can picture what it would be like to see his granddaughter a woman, speaking the strange language. He would like to live a little longer. He sits up and tells his wife, I'm not going to die or anything. Look how strong I am. Come here and I'll lift you like a lamb.

WHEN BEES WERE PEOPLE

Today's mystery has been submitted by
Bah: a great many winding roads,
the antelope herd marches along them all.
In between pages of sunlight, of predawn
darkness we march. These pages are quilted,
venous with blood, pressing against the
Rio Grande. Each strand of hair is rendered
with fine string. With no borders, the scene runs off
the page. Before we go on, let's gather some tea.
We know it tastes of time, neighboring flowers,
perhaps exhaust—it must set and dry.
Returning to a drowned man, a scene that smells
of leaves caught on a beach, fermenting, choking
the rocky shoals, muffling the lap.

The Tewas put on a dance honoring us,
dancing in our shirts, our hair,
our juniper wreathing their necks.
They smile, giggle, and we laugh, too,
indulging them. This last scene caws,
crows, actually. There's a barking man.
Give us back our tools, they say.
But these are our spindles—you've copied them.
The pages bloat unevenly here,
like water spilled on them, but we learn later
it sprouted from below, like blood, like lava.

We never ask: Do you dream about him?
Sit quietly after the movie.
We will get to your hands eventually.
We've been caught on a grinding

stone. Transformers stride through mountains,
bundling their wires each night.
Dry things accumulate: corn husks after harvest,
stacked high as two women read
a letter at its feet, a small hill tittering
with each breeze. Peaches on the canyon floor
set in a wide swath, deer meat darkening
on a cord, dust on picture frames, sheep droppings
in an empty corral. Newspapers, wool blankets,
polyester blankets, string-game string,
love life jokes: Boy, why don't you bring her home?
We promise we won't bite.

On the northern prairie the green grass dries yellow,
winter arriving. A man in a red headband yells,
You're in the wrong. The helmets with glass visors
march in, batons held high, striking. Mother, daughter,
father, son, you've got to feed them, give them corn.
Mother, father, little one. The deer hide them
under trees, dogs hide them under porches,
bears stray and must circle back.

BURNTWATER

T'ááłá'í

The Hopis rode through here built a fire from the oak and scrub cedar by the water the stream or pool now they call it Burntwater old women cooking around a fire. My great grandmother cooked in the summer sitting her knees on the ground skirt spreading out steel grill laid over an open fire in shade house bits of dough crusting her fingers. Now a young woman cooks potatoes over a blue flame on a stove in her city apartment. Dohí dohí before you light the acetylene torch to imagine fire shot from the sky my grandfather says before soldering bezel to silver bracelet loved one then sealing copper tubing with the same torch where the water's leak busted frozen last night. I say I don't know how to light a fire. Tightly wound nylon holds the gas when I work it now over a large piece but the solder doesn't flow metal blackens the thatched roof has caught spark my love. When I call my grandfather Shicheii he answers hello Shicheii we share the name. Blackest metal driest winter swing the sun low behind glass windows bottle green sculptures. I taped him set the tape recorder between us on the table loved one do you understand the red light to catch every inflection throat clearing gravel.

Naaki

He said   My uncle killed a man by the train tracks in winter another tribe or white man. Brought his pistol. Trains stopped for the night he had to pay or he had to run I don't know how he came to the ceremonies after that. From the police or from the killing. I'd see his face in the spring firelight as pairs of men and women danced a slow step around the fire wrapped in blankets the men wearing cowboy hats tilted up off their right ear so they could lean their heads close to the women. My uncle watched without watching sang without singing.

He said   She jumped off the cliff ran and jumped off the cliff. One soldier leapt from his horse to stop her my great grandmother said (we called her nihimá mother) to round us up set fire to our squash and melon fields smoke and ash like a summer fire but bitter in your heart. They found us campfire morning eating in the low piñons surrounded on horseback blue coats and brass buttons. Father shot first a snap in his neck bullet through forehead (she points) then fleeing rifle fire everyone dead and crying. Only my little mother and I brisk spring morning air cold in my throat cold and alive. We had almost made it to the canyon and shelter pine sap sticks to your teeth you taste its mint in every meal so they are the same food corn meal prairie dog yellow gourd use a strand of hair to pull pieces from crevices in your molars. Birds sing flit from tree to tree ahead of you as though it were any day. Come to the canyon's edge with the soldiers dragging us tied with rope. She breaks free. Where is the order of the sun indifferent meaning beats down on us she is fluid in these last steps the trees melting into rock at the edge and leaps. The sun is too bright everything flat and hard but she floats out. I miss her already. My little mother had stopped crying hours before she ran. I only heard my own tears. Now down. The sun's cords touching the rock at the edge meant she was gone.

He said We met at the Indian school. A dry Nevada with dry mountains where I make jewelry and signs high up on scaffolding red paint on the window pane shirt sleeves ripped off for dexterity yellow billboards on Route 66. The road goes on forever just like you said but Nevada I can't see anymore like my eye has cracked Nevada has fallen through every way I look. Six children so they could play with each other girls and one boy. In Flagstaff I see racism course through the coffee shops and schools. My brother opened a jewelry supply downtown. A prayer mountain on the north side Dook'o'oslííd we call it. They made their own games drew them on cardboard I said I'd paint them. The winters would have our truck spinning. I do not know what to say to my children. The road is hungry no matter how many signs you paint or politicians you work for their visions shouted in fists broken on mobs of our own people. Marriage is hard but that doesn't matter. Back to Gallup always inching closer to home but never reaching it we did it for you is what I say. Place with the big stone chimney they call Gamerco so many places we lived but always you children played where did you play? Where did you play? Turn off the tape turn off the tape turn off

Táá'

To play in the mist this is the most important thing. The house we sit in is a hogan attached to a four-walled home old magazines from the 80s and 90s on the bottom shelves. Old western movie video tapes under the TV in faded sleeves. If you drive north of the house on the dirt road over the rolling hills of piñon trees sagebrush and tea get down from your truck and walk west over low cacti the earth is sandy almost like the ocean's edge and water used to cover us you can still find white shells. You will find Burntwater grove of trees and cedars yellow sandstone emerging from the loose earth in places where the Hopis camped and let their horses drink. But in the house in the hogan where the skylight soft sun midmorning my grandfather cries and wipes tears from his face. His fingers look strange old and out of place against the face he rubs every morning to clear his eyes. I click the machine between us on the table slow but the echo of a gunshot and wait. We'll stop here today. To the south the freeway rumbles trucks haul refrigerators and pipes. On the windowsill the metal stamps and thin brushes sprout from rusted cans. It's cold. Even with the sun shining through the skylight I'll have to build a fire.

Chee Brossy was born in Chinle, Arizona, and grew up in Red Mesa, Arizona. He is Diné, originally from Lukachukai and Wheatfields, Arizona. He attended Dartmouth College, where he studied English and Native American Studies. His poetry and fiction have appeared in *Denver Quarterly*, *Sentence*, *Prairie Schooner*, *Red Ink Magazine* and elsewhere. He has worked as a reporter, basketball coach, English literature instructor, and fundraiser. He lives in New Mexico.